Memorias from the Beltway

Poems by
Mauricio Novoa

Red Salmon Arts/Red Salmon Press
Casa de Resistencia Books

FLOWERSONG
PRESS

A Joint Publication by FlowerSong Press and Red Salmon Arts in the United States of America. First Edition.

ISBN: 978-1-953447-09-8
Library of Congress Control Number: 2020950595

Cover Image: Oscar Novoa
Cover and Book Design: Jo Reyes-Boitel
Author Photo: Christine Castro

Red Salmon Arts is a 501(c)3 grassroots cultural arts organization, with an over thirty-year history of working with the indigenous neighborhoods of Austin. RSA is dedicated to the development of emerging writers and the promotion of Chicanx/@ Latinx/@/Native American literature, providing outlets and mechanisms for cultural exchange, and sharing in the retrieval of a people's cultural heritage with a commitment to social justice. Red Salmon Press, a program of Red Salmon Arts, is an editorial collective founded in the 1990s under the guidance of raúlrsalinas. RSP focuses on the retrieval of a people's literary heritage and the development of emerging young writers/readers through its publications.

This project is supported in part by the Cultural Arts Division of the City of Austin Economic Development Department.

Red Salmon Arts/Red Salmon Press
Casa de Resistencia Books

www.resistenciabooks.com

FLOWERSONG
PRESS
www.flowersongpress.com

c/s

Memorias from the Beltway

Poems by

Mauricio Novoa

To my family and Elena

To Abuelito Gregorio, Tío Agustín, and Jorge Perez-Rico

Preface

My first meeting with poet Mauricio Novoa was brief and unremarkable when Leticia Urieta, the co-director of Barrio Writers Austin and Pflugerville, introduced him to me as a new writing advisor for Barrio Writers in 2018. Leticia wanted to make sure that we connected because he was interested in volunteering for Red Salmon Arts (RSA). She believed he was the kind of person that would mesh well with RSA's often unorthodox, unruly, and unconventional practices of maintaining and sustaining our organization. Our relationship, indeed, evolved slowly and his patience and humility obscured an incredible fact about him—his talents as a poet and the veracity, clarity, and perception conveyed through his art.

Honestly, until a Café Libro in 2019, which spotlighted the stories, perspectives, and vision of Centroamericana/o/xs, I had not understood the power and significance of Novoa's poetry. Captivated both by the succinct and mindful fashion of the words, Novoa impressed upon this audience that his historia as an East Coast salvadoreño mattered. Additionally, his writings reveal why this all-too-often ignored voice is a critical part of literatura latinx of the United States.

Memorias from the Beltway is our first FlowerSong Press joint publication and the fourth Red Salmon Press full-length book dedicated to poetry illuminating the words and verses of nascent and established Chicanx/Latinx/Native American writers. Through our respective presses, we seek to rupture the hierarchical ways traditional modes of publishing insist upon only celebrating the works of the most widely-recognized or prolific authors and marginalizing the leading voices of Chicanx/Latinx/Native American/POC communities that are constantly innovating and creating. As Red Salmon Press, we are proud that Mauricio Novoa's provocative collection centers on the Central American experience. After over two decades, we are fulfilling a mandate to fully embrace that panoply of Chicanx/Latinx/Native American literary perspectives, which are integral to (re)defining who and what we are.

In this work, we are held at attention to listen and contend with themes of working class survivalism and ingenuity, spiritual tenacity, hip hop articulations, and el exilio via the poems of Mauricio, and his generation, to disrupt our own understandings of plural Latinidad. Poems such as "Happy Meals" to "Memorias from the Beltway" encapsulate nuances about salvadoreño masculinity through imagery of everyday forms of violence and resistance marking a thread between state-sponsored, insurgent, street sites for these expressions. Other pieces demonstrate a quiet invocation of memory, place, and intergenerationality that transports us to the perennial beats of the East Coast and prayers of abuelas. Last, the layers of familial strife, bonds, and strength depicted are a subtle ode to Mauricio's immigrant parents that is neither nostalgic nor cloying.

Twenty-five years after the publication the *East of the Freeway* by raúlrsalinas, *Memorias from the Beltway* is a much needed repuesta to the recollections, which raúl explores in another time of vast global, sociopolitical transformation and popular, grassroots uprisings. The intimate manner in which both Mauricio and raúl communicate the soulfulness of our rebellion through sparse and intentional words is certainly one point of commonality. Their love of la vida cotidiana is another moment of intersection. Undoubtedly, it is in these small acts of calling our existence that we persevere. *Memorias from the Beltway* implores us to dwell in these remembrances, mourn our losses, and honor the words we carve out as "lifelines."

—Lilia Rosas, Ph.D.
Executive Director, Red Salmon Arts
Osten, Tejaztlán, Otoño 2020

Table of Contents

When the lights shut off
and it's my turn to settle down
my main concern
promise that you will sing about me

-Kendrick Lamar

Dandelion Graves

after "War" by King Los

kids of the forgotten refugees, soil-less seeds
on the run from the barrel of a gun on their knees
ducking immigration until they're stationed as far as DC
or LA or the Bay, that was back in Reagan's 80s
when numbers shot up like a fiend, crack rock being steamed
in the apartment down the hallway from my mama's baby
but that wasn't the home that my parents made for me
Georgia Ave and Urbana in lily white Montgomery
except the Glenmont section was brown as Abuela's coffee
and the smell of asphalt would never wash off Papi
a good day was a meal that wasn't frijoles and cheese
so my dreams were drenched in leftover Chinese
but pull yourself and you'll succeed is the bullshit they would feed
so everyone drank piss until they couldn't see
cuz how's a kid like me supposed to think when it's engraved
the only future that awaits is a dandelion grave

Blur

The baby dreams in its stroller.
The library's air conditioning cradles
their skin against the Texas heat before their mom holds
them gently on her shoulder to browse
on a Tuesday morning. She'll banter
with a couple she met in the picture books, as casual
conversations of weekend events, the $8
Peanut butter and jelly sandwich at the downstairs café, and
immigration ease between them. One will say, "That's what happens
when you come here illegally," as another
says, "But those poor children." Words mingle
into something like middle ground, and they depart as easy
as they came together into the uncomfortable
afternoon, that burns a baby's feet a highway away as they stand
in a cage searching a blurred world for anyone
who might say, "Aquí estoy."

If I Lose Mami Tonight

may the cold in their hearts drop
below 20 degrees so their blood becomes
the blue life they say matters.

May their soulless eyes look
into the same eternity that holds hostage
any moment it chooses – school, work, a birthday party –
and stare into it trying to see if it's their name
etched onto the bullet.

May their nightmares be the pulse
of their presidents and the nursery rhymes
in their children's classrooms and may their safety
and hope be worth the pennies dulled
on scratch-off tickets.

If I lose Mami tonight
may I finally lose faith in the olive branch
because the wood is a burning cross
on government property. May words
stop being my fists so I can feel
a nose crack on my knuckles. May my nature
melt away, void like they would Mami's green card,
so I may do something to make ICE break.
But maybe if I lose Mami tonight,
I hear her say "cuidate" in pouring water
as it shrinks and cracks ice cubes in a glass.

Pennies for the Pulpit

I.

The stairs become Annapurna
turning coughs into gasps.
I peak and find Abuela
in the kitchen
after pulling my body
across the floor
as if both legs
were shot, no
words between failed
asthma breaths
so she calls Papi
then begins to pray.
Finally the air dam
breaks, a drop
of wind sneaks into
my esophagus, followed
by a rush of life.
"Gracias a dios," she says,
but I was reading
the bible before
my lungs closed.

II.

Every few minutes, Ms. Erickson would herd us
into the corner of the portable where the least light shines
so we aren't tempted to poke through the blinds.
The lights would go off because we hope bullets
also get lost in the dark. Through whimpers

sneak "I want my mommy"s and calls to angels
to bring us protection, but if angels were absent
from the Michael's parking lot, would a divine sword block
the sniper scope from our view?

III.

If Jesus' blood is fermented
grapes then the holy spirit is stronger 80 proof
in soda, all smiles down to my grape Kool-Aid
shirt. Hell is a small hospital room with white
walls and a snake feeding from my stomach,
smaller serpents become extensions of my veins as souls
both end and begin in levels above me.
Dull fluorescent lights became holy
when they never turned off.

IV.

Abuela's middle-aged friends, all named Hermana,
sit in a line in the front of the basement
of the Sagrado Corazon, where homeless men
take communion on the sidewalk. I'm seated
in the front row as the priest goes behind each woman,
his hand over their heads as he bellows what sounds
like a prayer. The women quiver enough to make their chairs
rumble during sermon, their lungs erupt
into sacred hymns, I couldn't stop
crying - finding solace with the St. Ides prophets
sitting on their concrete Tempurpedics,
crackling with the winter wind
behind their baptism of soil and urine.

The Food

Poetry, like bread, is for everyone.
-Roque Dalton

In assigned readings, sentences we could understand
were as scarce as rainbow-colored salads
in our refrigerators. While the cover
of every book was like a mirror
for our English teachers, for us it was a cracked window.

Stories of characters based on
shit we would be shot or arrested for
ring true as prayers
for saviors that grace our necks
but never the court or hospital rooms.

Standards for syntax follow patterns
out of our natural rhythms, ensuring
our words are always dissonant
so we scratched the records

into beats in our time signatures,
Stretched our sonnets by a few
couplets, and took education
out of outdated books like seeds
out of infertile soil, and turned school hallways
and notebooks into gardens.

Aristotle biting an apple can cruise
down the street in a '64 if it's spit
on a DJ Quik beat, scratched

in a book banned in Arizona,
or tattooed on a forearm, but that won't
be served on a tray in the school
cafeteria. Those words come fresh
in pupusas and red Kool-Aid.

Birthday Party in the Orchards

after a photograph taken by Jorge Perez-Rico

The boy takes a break from playing
with all his little amigos and primos
so the photographer can freeze the first day
of his 6th year. To cope with the high demands
of his celebrity, he rewards himself
with a juice pouch, sweating with the remains
of the ice cubes that held it before the boy
made it his co-star for the still.

Some of the juice drips down to his jorts,
but they'll dry once he goes back
to running around in his chanclas
in the apple orchard his parents worked
under the Adams County sun from tree to tree,
reaching for every ripe Macintosh or Red Delicious
to fill their buckets because their wages are measured in bushels.

All those apples sit watching the party
they paid for, shaded in their crates
as the guests sweat from the games of tag
and the boy's parents sweat from the tinga steaming
from the silver olla sweating orange.
They watch everyone enjoy the free afternoon
before they clock in to their outdoor office,
one hundred paces away from their beds.

Happy Meals

Humble pie comes in McDonald's
boxes in apple and pumpkin, but luxury
is Oreo McFlurry's on pay day,
checks alternating bi-homie,
me one Friday, Zach another,
Moyer a Monday, Brandon the next.
Mami ain't home 'til 7, but I get hungry
by 3 and my last meal was the night before
so Daniel's $5 is split 5 ways
with me, JC, Miles and Ismail on a mission
for McChickens, splitting Ismail's back seat,
skinniest one is the seatbelt.
After we hoop in the park, post-game stretches
are turning quarters into 4-person meals,
Taco Bell burritos dank as Zach's bowl
perfume Puente's mini coop with Grade D beef perfume
as we're rolling through Maryland's richest county
wondering who'll have the 5 for tomorrow's dinner.

J's

I couldn't do Payless anymore -
no more K-Mart, Target, or anywhere
else selling cheap-ass knock off, off brand,
looks-like-mama-sewed-em-together shoes.
When everyone else rocked the Air Force 1s,
I rolled in my $20 Shaqs
that the upper echelon in the hallways
of Parkland Middle School always stepped
on cuz they weren't shit anyways.
But when I saw those Red-Black-and White
Air Jordans on the bargain rack for $80,
I had to have them.

I walked through Glenmont still JC Penny-
bargain-bin fly, but with my J's on I could drift
without fiends asking me for a dollar
for a McDouble then laughing cuz they could tell
I was as hungry as they were. I could bounce
up the block to the bops in my headphones
like a ball before we bought it flat

from the thrift store. I could feel like I could walk
as far as I wanted, and I'd never walk home barefooted.

The Positive Rhyme

after "The Intro About Nothing" by Wale

I wasn't born to be better at anything than anybody
Mama made me to breathe as much air as I could carry, call me

the heir to bare minimums, only enjoy luxuries in interims
beans and French bread for lunch, so in school we were the miserables

But if I leave nothing behind except pennies and mediocrity
Let Abuela quote one of my lines like coffee shop bros quote Socrates

Let my brothers hold the heart I couldn't give them when they needed
When all we had were rocks to chew on as babies teething

Hands bleeding from scratching the cracking skin from cold weather
Waiting to thaw our shivering digits out like some frozen chicken tenders

So let Papi warm the overtime plow truck with one of my open letters
Let Abuelo feel my rhythms vibrate from his resting bones up to a heaven

of my own making, no ratings or shaming shading my judgement
Mama's son shone even if he's not the brightest he's not the dumbest

Chessmen

My feet drag on the sidewalk,
heavy from the after school
May sun that follows me home
and heavier from the absence
of breakfast or lunch. Cafeteria lines
the length of the school are sandwiched into an hour
and my parents' hungry wallets that feed
four boys make this routine, but luckily
Zach had $2 for a side-cart cheeseburger
he was willing to share with a group of four.

The refrigerator offers only eggs and milk,
and frijoles made days ago still wait
on a pan, so I settle for cereal and join my 3 brothers
on the couch, our bowls the only things full
in the house. But when Mami gets home from work
at 7, she pulls out a bag of Chessmen that lists
more ingredients than dishes we've tried.
We eat Kings and Queens like cake,
tomorrow's lunch lost in the crumbs.

Wu Tang is for the Children[2]

or, *In Defense of Teaching Hip Hop in School and Removing the Parental Advisory Sticker: Sijo*

Would you debate the possible side effects of the medicine
in an epi-pen or the physical harm of CPR
as your kid's lungs close in their quick-chilling chest?

For Childhood Heroes

When dinners are hot
dogs and refried
beans, dreams boil
in dirty saucepans.

Unwashed
hands taught me how
to drink without getting sick,
how to digest the nutrients
in ingredients meant to kill
us.

My life past 18 rests
in palms that will never be clean,
and I wonder if later
I'll remember them for carrying
me or be disgusted by the filth.

18

for Alejandro

They keep calling you
"a man." Every newspaper
begins with your adulthood,
a technicality, though you're still
not allowed a beer but a perfect
excuse to only devote 7 lines
to the absence of a brown body. Edited out
is the logic for their own children: they're
young, they're kids. They're given
Dateline specials and search parties
when something happens. You, however,
are just an Aspers man, one paragraph
the only searchlight, only turned on
by the people who love you, busy
work for a staff writer who only
had to fill up time to get to 5pm, when
they can go home and see their kids.

Jumper

You take the first step,
dribble slow like your bus
isn't coming in 20 minutes,
then snap like a rat in the kitchen
when the lights come on, drive
down the lane for a layup so wide
open the park is empty,
and miss.

You go for the lonely rebound but jam
your finger into the ball so you feel
like a cartoon, set
your feet for the jumper, Ray Allen
form, but this is no Game 6 so you get
only air, not like Mike.

Every hit to the rim
is like a hit to your elbow so it isn't tucked,
a hit to your hand so it doesn't follow through,
a cloud to your rainbow so you don't arch
and it's just like everything else.
Close but not enough.

Then your corner 3 glides through the net,
falling as perfect as a drop of water
from a leaf in a Nikon photo,
smooth as the sweat from the tip
of your nose.
Then you miss your bus.

Memorias from the Beltway

I.

The bullet entered Romero's chest
at Mass. A week later, heaven repaid
with a plague of rifle rounds through bomb smoke
at his funeral. Papi was 13, old enough to hold a rifle,
like his friends who brought AK's
to birthday parties because military uniforms
made skin bulletproof. He watched friends
open friend's veins on schoolyard playgrounds
and hid from tanks taking his class'
roll call. While Abuela sang hymns, he wrote love poems to prove hearts
with bullet holes can still beat. Abuelo bounced first
from San Salvador to the District, almost
a decade after hope for the hungry bled onto bread. After BPD
released "Stop The Violence," Abuelo sent
for Abuela and Papi, who's first DC job
was at a gas station. A week later, he learned guns
have siblings, a familiar cold on the back of his neck
as the register was emptied.

II.

From their county-stamped cruiser, eyes like streetlamps
surveil every movement down Urbana Drive and Flack

Street with a bullet
for anything they can't see. And like the street

craters under their
wheels, the grass in between them and my
house depresses from new suspects,

new shivers from cold cuffs, new questions
of walking away alive. There's even

a cavity in the grass from all the Yankee
fitted brims pummeled for whatever invented offense,

barely missing my sidewalk.

III.

but sometimes life is carne asada, drunk
uncles, and soccer balls soaring
over fences into neighbor's yards
who don't give a fuck how many
times we have to hop to get them back.
They say "que tal" too. That's vecino for
"play that shit all night if you want. No noise
complaints here."

IV.

Watch maps fly farther
  than our dreams. Watch children
try to find El Salvador between
  Red Line stations on Metro
directories. Watch fathers and mothers
  escape borders but their children
never leave the Beltway. Now watch
  their older cousins, in Yankee fitted
caps, a 24 Laker jersey,
  and a Cowboys case on their phones
with a Messi background, take us
  to New York, Detroit, Compton,
and watch us take notebooks and try
  to bring them back to the Beltway.

V.

Squad cars roll slow, heavy
like tanks leaving imprints on our sense
of safety. You
would think the 13 year old
sitting in the backseat had brought
a rifle and aimed it at someone's chest,
but no. He set off a stink bomb.
No one died that day, though some
who watched him in cuffs will years later,
but at least 64 bullets in 4 sidearms
stop our hearts and beg
to open them, rattling the clip,

staring longingly up the barrel, praying
to leave brim imprints in front
of this middle school. And we
stare with tunnel vision past the flashing
lights at the streetlamp, praying
we pass under in an hour heading home,
notebooks without bullet holes.

VI.

We hit the courts with three
hours of sun left because we wanted
to go home with our shoes. Just as
scrub league was set to commence,
two guys asked to play. We didn't want
to embarrass ourselves, but we said
yes anyways. We made sure to split
them up in case they were any good.
Who remembers how anyone played,
but we shot through time quick
enough. One of the two said he just
got home the week before, it didn't matter
how long he was gone. Or why. No one
gave him a scholarship to ball anywhere, and they
made sure no one ever would, even if he
could or couldn't dunk on us every play.
Even if his GPA was higher than our
points per game. Most of us never leave,
but teammates stolen from us outnumber
our hundreds of missed shots. We never
got a rematch.

VII.

Saturday nights were sitting in the corner
of a room in Beltsville as 15 cousins play Mario Kart,
writing to 2Pac and Game beats playing
over the chorus of Tio's and Tia's shit talk
in the living room. The paper is passed around
because they want a follow up from last week's
"Freestyle #3"

MD's MC, that's what they used to call me
When I was writing my first lyrics at the age of 13
Wackest shit you ever heard, but in my head I was the best in the world
But I was a broken faucet with no flow and lines cheesier than Utz curls

Summer breezes were sleeping over
at the Virginia cousin's house, knowing that waking
up the next morning is watching G-Unit videos
on his family computer, and showing him
a notebook full of Nas imitations

Ignite the fire and fan the flames
Let it burn every time your tongue mentions my name
Far too dope to let you motherfuckers take me in vein
But you'll never smoke me, got everybody choking

A normal day is a cold Glenmont basement
Papi gone for days plowing snow for sub zero
paychecks after presents, Mami on the metro
next to the white people who's $230 a night toilet
she just cleaned, me looking at rejection notices feeling like Kanye, like

Damn

Is everyone else
that much better than
me?[3]

VIII.

Kevin Durant was drafted in 2007
by the Oklahoma City Thunder because
he practiced his jumper since he was little,
with coaches correcting his mistakes,
watching Jordan and Iverson on TV.
So what if instead of reading Lord of the Flies and Robert Frost
every year, someone assigned Sonia Sanchez?
If someone showed me how to paint an empty fridge
with words instead of the multiple fonts F's come in,
would I still be waiting for a rookie contract?

IX.

I'm not supposed to take
it personal, but it feels like my pockets
were stolen just as I thought I was about to
fill them. Was all this practice
just bench pressing with no weights, like Pops

getting ahead in amerikkka. We were counterfeiting
meal tickets in our high school hallways,
I got cocky enough to think I could forge
a plane ticket out of rhymes and hope
boiled from lotto scratch-off dust,

my ass still covered in the gravel from Mami's stoop.
Hanging hip hop posters was like screwing
in a small bulb in a dark auditorium, Rapsody's voice the sound
you follow to find the light switch.
I still chug beer from the bottle
craving a sip of the milk rent bills drank up, still
trying to stop reading "No" as "Quit," still standing

on Pac's shoulders trying to get hang time
like Jordan instead of an Earl
Manigault rebound, because we're

born with loaded rifles into echo chambers
where everyone yells "Shoot!"

and the music jammed the gun.

Motherfuckin' Trees

are beautiful. White kids had tree
houses and I had a swing until Papi made a drive
way. The bits of forest were good for forgetting
we'd never go camping. Or see the mountains
on National Geographic magazines in doctor's
offices. I hate going outside but the sun
can't do shit to shade under a thick trunk
and a bunch of green-ass leaves. Clearly
I don't write enough about nature or else
this'd be an ode a tree could tell the wind
on those breezy Maryland September days
I'm so far away from, but Mami didn't
let me stay outside too much if no one
was watching, and they were usually
too busy to watch.

Old Head

Papi always talks about how thin
he was –how he used to touch both hands
on the backboard and run soccer fields
until the sun hid behind the volcanoes in El Salvador.

The photograph shows some truth –
a young man in skinny jeans and a leather jacket,
no more than 130 lbs. – almost a whole person
smaller than the man
who tells me I should be more active
so my weight doesn't follow me to his age.

Me and my brothers crack up at the stories
the old heads tell around the table
when they get together to reminisce on the glory years –
before back pains, knee surgeries, children –
when they ran wild as wolves,
even though we caught snaps of the leash
when we came home after the moon.

1st Day of School

In his asphalt cologne

Papi hugged me goodbye.

His words exhausted

like choking smoke,

as he looked for a bathroom

to let his eyes flow out

like he did on rent days.

The Gold Year

We passed a children's detention center,
just parallel to Desirable
Drive, on our way to DC for Abuelo y Abuela's
50th wedding anniversary. Boda de Oro. 29
of those years spent sweating
into an unkind economy, but not before
Abuela y Mami were stopped in Brownsville.

Mami said they were detained
3 days, and every day they were given free
time outside. On the 3rd day, they just walked
away. Then they flew. But hate here is grounded
and grown, like a gold statue made to survive time.

Calluses

Mami's feet were a Weller Road Elementary
census, each callus a Spanish speaking teacher.
Because she cleaned hotel rooms, I was almost switched
into an ESOL class, even though she had Mr. Rogers
tutor me to English fluency. We got a mirror
in our bedroom when she got more than Univision
to watch at 7pm, home from work eating at the table
by herself – 4 boys sleeping in the same bed but meals
in whatever hole they found or made. Some nights
I rubbed her feet after pulling out her canas, her soles
blistered with each country she left behind, each quarter
she got as a raise for promotions, each vacation and conference
she tidied up without a tip. When she accidentally
hit the remote and it switched to the English channels,
the characters only said "Hola" when they were scrubbing
a toilet. That might explain why she always fell asleep
halfway through a movie. And why 6 weekend tequilas
were what made her dance then pull me in, dragging
my brick feet to cumbia. And why whatever
school loans didn't cover went on her credit card. I got
my first callus on my left toe when I started working
with Spanish speaking students, one for every teacher
they might have had that talked like us. One for every
dirty mirror I stood in front of as I shaved. One for every stomach
pump after drinking like a grown-ass, hard-working-for-
worthless-pennies woman that made Mami the first thing
I saw when I woke up and had work that Monday.
But because of the 12 she'd put on my ass for being a baboso,
I may never get another.

The Bee

flies through the hole
        in the bug screen we made
running away as Oscar, Gerardo, Dani, and I took turns chasing
        each other with dead crickets and cockroaches
and Barney plush dolls that gave us
        nightmares and Gerardo paused and ran
towards me to avoid the stinger that
        might get caught in his nose again

he rushes through me into the kitchen
        I follow and slide the door to a slam
the same force as when Abuelo's parakeet flapped past crosses
        and grocery store calendars behind me its beak
knocked before its body thumped the air vent
        on the floor and Abuelo's lowered gaze pulled
my fear into earth where we buried the pajarito

and I hope the bee doesn't knock
        where we hide because Abuelo's tea
would taste forever bitter and only dead
        crickets and cockroaches would sing summer songs.

Can't Afford A Triolet

Roaches cover my sheets
and frijoles. Is all we have
filled with holes and expired last week?
Roaches cover my sheets
as I try not to write about concrete
after burning blunts to the clip 'til I gag.
Now roaches cover my sheets,
and frijoles is all we have.

Tears for Gregorio

I.

The final date on the white board was July 13th, 2014.
Your dough belly stopped rising
with the EKG line, neither you or Abuela,
glasses buried on my shoulders, could rate your pain.

II.

You hold the trumpet to your lips
in between National Orchestra practices,
flexing your fingers for the Sunday crowd
before they are starved of their faith.
I imagine that's how you impressed your first wife.

III.

My hands covered my face like I'm praying –
Shit, I just didn't want anyone to see me cry
like I used to when you took me to church.
They said prayers over people's heads
and I felt more scared than blessed.

IV.

The crowd fills the stadium to see Club Deportivo Marte,
but all those ticket and pupusa sales
never make it to you or your teammates' pockets.
You skip the stretching since you walked 6 miles
to get to the game so my dad could have the bus fare
for school. Those 90 minutes shooting in front of all of
El Salvador soothed your nerves before you have to run
from the U.S. camo team. I imagine this is how you
impressed your second wife, Abuela.

V.

The last time you could raise your left arm
I was raising a red cup in a piss-stained basement.
For months you were teased with the idea of life,
stuck in front of the TV
whenever you weren't eating or sleeping.
At least your last month was on a World Cup year.

VI.

You looked a lot younger right before they closed the casket,
the wrinkles from your glasses to your beard so smoothed
it could have been me sleeping before school, waiting
for you to wake me up to shower.
I couldn't follow the path of your pain,
so maybe that's what it'll look like
when my pain is gone,
when I can believe you're somewhere watching
over me. Maybe I do believe that?
I really want you to see that first book
is dedicated to you.
Love,
Molichin.

"I Just Called to Say I Love You"[4]

Hola abuela, llama Mauricito.

Our last conversation was timestamped about 3 months,
an area code, and a few hundred 'I'll call this week's' ago,
but she answers with the same *mi'jo, como estas?*

I promised a weekly delivery,
instead my route followed el viajero
so I was delayed a bit, but the signal is stronger
now that I've shaved a time zone between us.

Ya estas conociendo muchos lugares,
she says from her daughter's house
in San Salvador, where I used to beg Papi
to let me go in the summers when we drove
to Reagan at 5am to see her and Abuelo
off, where yuca grew fresh down the road
and Oscar Romero gave his parting sermon
at a church nearby and he told her to stop
asking him stupid questions.

She only had tickets for two, and Papi
only had enough for parking.

I tell her about the book I submitted poems
to, and she says *mándame una copia;*
She didn't hear me say I have to wait
to hear back first, but she also pre-ordered
my first CD when I was figuring out how to hold
my guitar. I say hopefully I get lucky,

she says *primero Dios.*

We end with the promise of a text
on my birthday, and I wipe
my phone dry to hang up the call.

Victory Lap [5]

for Nipsey Hussle

The victory lap is supposed to come at the end,
once every opponent has watched you cross
checkered banners and the memories of moments
that should've ended the race before it began carry
your feet to a point where you can finally cruise
and just enjoy your time. You deserved to enjoy time
because 33 years wasn't even a warmup
and most of that was spent in a marathon and I wonder
sometimes why we miss people we never knew
then I remember when I saw you claim victory
and have a champion's parade from Crenshaw
to the Mayan ruins in your debut. You didn't know
this was gonna be the final finish line, but you made the crowd
watch you celebrate, and celebrate with you,
because victory isn't running your last lap, but running
as far as you did when the start felt further than the finish line.

Abuela Sestina

Abuelo would wake us up, Abuela would take us to the school
bus stop every morning before her breakfast, the drive
only 30 seconds but her knees couldn't go as far as her glasses.
Before every drive, she twisted her right-hand fingers into a cross,
praying for a safe return to enjoy her frijoles, pan,
crema, and platanos with her husband and birds.

She always made us grind up moldy food for the birds
next to her garden of tomates y jalapeños. It was one of the after-school
jobs she gave us, along with weeding and sorting Avon products. Pan
dulce y café were unfinished on the table as she'd drive
me from Maryland to DC to viajeros and cross-
city sales. More than once, she dragged me to the stained-glass

Sagrado Corazon for misa, where the prayers over the glass
with Jesus' blood scared me like the bird
and swine flu talk in the hallways. It never got across
that maybe we'd never share the same schools
of thought, that the more she made me pray, the more she'd drive
me out of the pew. If it did, she drowned her worries in a pan

of oil for pasteles, or memories of the Pan
Am flight to DC in the 80s from Reagan's broken-glass
San Salvador. Sometimes when we waited in the drive-
way for her Ford Focus to heat up, covered in snow and bird
shit, platicaba de cipotes that belonged in school
yards with guns their height crossing

their chests and how Oscar Romero once became cross

with her, cackling as she remembers a deadpan
reprimand from our martyr, and I nodded and said uh-huh as I schooled
myself to do whenever I only understand a half-glass
of story streaming from her memory. I wish, like the pajarito
tweets Abuelo studied for "hungry" and "need exercise," I had the drive

to learn this language that thrives a 3 day drive
from home grown loroco and guayaba. But she made me cross
Georgia Avenue to the CVS to translate to the Larry Bird
looking pharmacist about her medicine anyways, and never panned
pronunciations. It's like at night when she removes her teeth and glasses,
says te quiero mucho even after we fuck up prayers she tried to Sunday
School

into our bird brains though it feels like it drives
a pair of school scissors through her heart that we don't wear a cross
when we're told to. She stays warm like pan de gallina, knowing
the rest of the world looks to blanket us with fiberglass.

Marine

Recruitment in Wheaton is picking
dandelions – no one wants these weeds
so bundle them and let them die
somewhere foreign with no water,
still invasive but you tell them
they're beautiful. You see their
brown skin like rat fur that makes children
scream because you told them how disgusting
they are, full of disease. But they're useful.
Give them the gun you pointed at their parents'
chests in their old casas de carton[6] and teach
them to shoot with a hand over their heart.
Teach them it isn't wrong to die for red and blue
bandanas as long as they're stitched in the right
patterns. Win-win – they catch a bullet
after handing out 100 more, and their mamis
and papis catch a pause in their heartbeat,
wondering if standing for national anthems
will keep their son's body from falling.

Dandelion Bouquet

When I was little and wanted to show Mami
I loved her, I picked her flowers. The bright, pretty yellow
ones that seemed to grow everywhere – in gardens, on the lawn,
between cracks in the sidewalk and cracks in between beer bottles.
They shone to me even in storms that brought trees
down to earth. They came back every time they were cut
so I could always find them when they were needed, though it was sad
that they always died the day I gave them to her.
But she'd never throw them away – she kept them next
to the sink as she made tortillas or pancakes until I brought more.
How long that was depended on how long it took
to come down from my room, from where I kicked out my brothers
and sat alone crying for reasons even I didn't know. But however long
that was, I knew I could come down eventually, and there she was -
waiting for more flowers.

Meta

is a word fools
like me used when making
fun of dumb ass
intellectuals who talk a lot
but don't say shit: Poets.

Harvard motherfuckers invading
our high schools in their Trojan Horses.
Books that if we lost
we couldn't graduate until the fee –
Ivy League chump change –
was collected. Poetry –

"roses are red, violets are blue,
I am the lonely moon walking
along the river to fly to you."

You feel me?

Probably as much
as I feel Frost or Dunn
after rereading one line ten times
before clocking out. I wanna be Big
Pun, *dead in the middle of little Italy*
little did we/ know we riddled two middle
men who didn't do diddley,[7]
not Octavio Paz, *like clear water lying*
on closed eyes/In a tree's shadow.[8] I wanna be
Wheaton, 4 year old Shaq's trying to be

Jordan's but the stitches snap by the next
morning, not Harvard, boat shoes
used on grass soaked in red wine.

Cardi B and Shakespeare might have both
rhymed and bounced over lines, but I can
only quote one back to my English teacher,
and if I'm lucky enough to get my book lost
by a self-doubting wordsmith, hopefully the words won't be.

Ambitions

I can't afford to fall flat like in summer hoops
Knocked down onto the asphalt in the payless shoes
That my folks gave up dentist trips to lace me in
Just to scoff on shots barely grazing rim
But I felt craziest when I had thoughts of making it
Past the landmarks of the neighborhood they raised me in
But what good was it for me to up and leave home
If I can't make myself worth at least my parent's bank loans
And my words aren't the equity that my family needed
For some central heating and a house that didn't look depleted
When roaches were in my cereal and mice under the sink
They still looked for any reason to laugh and make the glasses clink
So if my words were a lifeline when escape felt the farthest
Then my life lives in these lines, and I got bars, I promise
And on my mama I'mma make a meter mean a reader
Feels her breathing in the spaces she said she'd see us

Thoughts in Flight

I look out of a head-sized window
30,000 feet above the apartment where I spent
my first Christmas without my family.
Clouds tickle the plane like grass
around a kid's head as they lay
on the field after being slide tackled for the ball
in a pick-up soccer game and nearly rolling
into the previous night's Corona bottles
so I can imagine the children
staring up from the front steps of their houses,
wishing one day to ride the only shooting stars
we've ever seen, back when the world was flat
and ended at Georgia Ave and Randolph Road.

Endnotes

[1] Reference to lyrics from "Boyz-N-The-Hood" by Eazy-E and N.W.A.

[2] Quote from Ol' Dirty Bastard from the 1998 Grammy Awards.

[3] Reference to lyrics from Kanye West's song "Touch the Sky."

[4] Reference to Stevie Wonder song of the same name.

[5] Reference to Nipsey Hussle's final album of the same name.

[6] Reference to song by Los Guaraguao of the same name.

[7] Line from Big Pun's song "Twinz (Deep Cover '98)."

[8] Line from Octavio Paz' poem "In Her Splendor Islanded."

Acknowledgements

Many thanks to the editors and staff of the following journals and anthologies where these pieces were previously published, sometimes in earlier versions.

Journals
Latino Book Review, "The Food"
La Horchata Zine, "Happy Meals" and "For Childhood Heroes"
Blue Mesa Review, "Calluses"
Petigru Review, "The Bee"
Acentos Review, "Marine" and "Jailhouse Library"

Anthologies
The Wandering Song: Central American Writing in the United States, "Dandelion Graves" and "J's".
The BreakBeat Poets Vol. 4: LatiNext, "Dandelion Graves" and "Jailhouse Library".

Thanks

First, I want to thank Lilia Rosas and Red Salmon Arts for giving my work a home and embracing me during my time in Austin. I learned so much from spending time in the bookstore, meeting so many different people and hearing the words of the amazing writers that passed through. Thank you, Jo Reyes-Boitel, for your time, wisdom, and patience in editing. I had no idea what this process was like and you made it easy and comfortable. And thank you, Edward Vidaurre and FlowerSong Press, for believing in this book.

Thank you to my professors and classmates at Queens University of Charlotte, where many of these poems made their first appearance and grew, especially Ada Limón, Marcus Jackson, Cathy Smith-Bowers, and Morri Creech who gave me extensive feedback and Fred Pond for the continued correspondence and friendship.

I also want to give my love to the artists who created the soundtrack that inspired my work and who's mastery of words I'm always trying to reach, which includes Tupac, Biggie, Nas, Rapsody, Kendrick Lamar, Nitty Scott, Lauryn Hill, Wale, DMX, Aaliyah, Jay-Z, Alicia Keys, Big Pun, Juanes, Bone Thugs, Cardi B, Chamillionaire, Javier Zamora, Danez Smith, Aja Monet, Natalie Diaz, Hanif Abdurraqib, Martin Espada, Franny Choi, Jamila Woods, Yesika Salgado, Elizabeth Acevedo, Fatimah Asghar, and countless others.

To my family, Mami, Papi, my brothers Gerardo, Dani, and Oscar (who drew the amazing cover art), Abuelita Ruth, Abuelita Elena, Abuelito Julio, all my tios and tias and cousins (especially Elmer, Veronica, Emma, Vanessa, Cindy, Kevin, Roy, Jesse, Wendy, Charlie, Lovely, Claudia, Julio, Flor, Eduardo, Edgar, Nydia, Marcos, Juan) for the support and love all my life and for reading everything from middle school until now. To all my people in the DMV, Gettysburg and Austin who have shown love and friendship, way too many to name (but especially Brandon, Zach, Moyer, Miles, and Huddy for the years-long and still going friendships). To Professor Melton and Dean Curry for the guidance on a campus where I would've been lost without it. To Brenda for hyping me up all over Twitter and pushing me to be more visible as a Central American writer. To Victoria, Vicki, Elias, and Jose Roque, for making Gettysburg feel like home and showing me love I needed. And to Abuelito Gregorio, Tío Agustín, and Jorge, I hope I made you proud.

And finally, to my rock, my main editor, my support, my partner, Elena, thank you for everything. None of this happens without you, and I can't say enough how much you mean to me.

About the Author

Photo Credit: Christine Castro

Mauricio Novoa is from Glenmont, Maryland, but is currently based in Austin, Texas. He received his MFA in Creative Writing at Queens University of Charlotte. Novoa's poems have been published in the anthology *The Wandering Song: Central American Writing in the United States, The Petigru Review, Acentos Review, Blue Mesa Review, Latino Book Review* and the anthology *The BreakBeat Poets Vol. 4: LatiNext.*

www.mauricionovoa.com

www.ingramcontent.com/pod-product-compliance
Lightning Source LLC
Chambersburg PA
CBHW021745190726
48288CB00009B/3160

* 9 7 8 1 9 5 3 4 4 7 0 9 8 *